Gourd Puppets and Dolls

C. Angela Mohr

Schiffer Publishing Ltd

4880 Lower Valley Road, Atglen, PA 19310

Other Schiffer Books by C. Angela Mohr
Making Gourd Ornaments, 978-0-7643-2716-2, $12.95
Gourd Art Basics, 978-0-7643-2829-9, $14.95
Historic Gourd Crafts, 978-0-7643-2830-5, $14.95

Other Schiffer Books on Related Subjects
Decorating Gourds: Carving, Burning, Painting and More, 0-7643-1312-6, $14.95
Gourd Crafts, 978-0-7643-2825-1, $14.95

Schiffer Books are available at special discounts for bulk purchases for sales promotions or premiums. Special editions, including personalized covers, corporate imprints, and excerpts can be created in large quantities for special needs. For more information contact the publisher:

Published by Schiffer Publishing Ltd.
4880 Lower Valley Road
Atglen, PA 19310
Phone: (610) 593-1777; Fax: (610) 593-2002
E-mail: Info@schifferbooks.com

For the largest selection of fine reference books on this and related subjects, please visit our web site at
www.schifferbooks.com
We are always looking for people to write books on new and related subjects. If you have an idea for a book please contact us at the above address.

This book may be purchased from the publisher.
Include $3.95 for shipping.
Please try your bookstore first.
You may write for a free catalog.

In Europe, Schiffer books are distributed by
Bushwood Books
6 Marksbury Ave.
Kew Gardens
Surrey TW9 4JF England
Phone: 44 (0) 20 8392-8585; Fax: 44 (0) 20 8392-9876
E-mail: info@bushwoodbooks.co.uk
Website: www.bushwoodbooks.co.uk
Free postage in the U.K., Europe; air mail at cost.

Designed by RoS
Type set in New Baskerville BT

ISBN: 978-0-7643-2868-8
Printed in China

Dedication

This book is dedicated to my mother, Mary Mohr, who used to meet with her friends to make monkey sock dolls. I remember them cutting up brown and white socks with red toes and then rearranging the pieces before sewing them back together into monkey shapes. When I make gourd dolls, I like to think I use my mother's talents, skills, and enthusiasm for creative endeavors...a mother's legacy to her grateful daughter.

What's Inside!

Introduction

Usually a gourd book concentrates on only gourds, paint, and perhaps some woodworking skills. How wonderful to combine the two interesting and creative worlds of fabrics and gourds for folks not necessarily captivated by woodworking tools or gourd dust! You do not have to be a great seamstress, or even a great artist. The simplest sewing and art skills can produce a wide variety of dolls and then, with some strings, puppets.

I suspect gourd dolls were common at one time when toys were considered a luxury, perhaps even inaccessible due to the many miles to town shops. They were probably products of leftover household bits and pieces.

The basic sewing and finishing skills we use in this book can apply to small dolls or to bigger, lap-sized dolls. In fact, the size of the doll or puppet will be determined by the size of the gourd that becomes the head. For small dolls, I use mini-bottleneck gourds. For larger dolls I use regular, full-sized bottleneck gourds, also called birdhouse gourds. These gourds have a distinctive pinched-in area in the middle that makes a natural curve for the neck of a doll body.

This is an old gourd doll I bought.

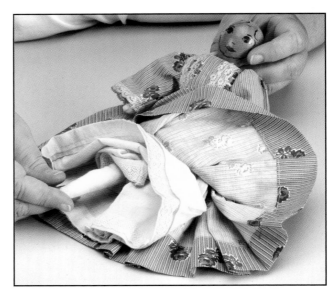

A bottleneck gourd was cut for the head and attached to a cloth body.

These gourds are called bottleneck, or birdhouse, gourds. The miniature gourds, though substantially smaller than the full-sized gourd, are fully mature. A pronounced center curve is what we want to have since it will form the neck of our doll and hold the body in place.

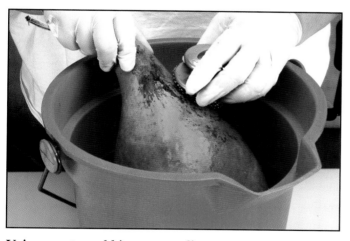

Chapter One:

To clean a gourd, put it into a tub of water. Warm is nice because it softens the surface debris faster, but tap water will work too. This gourd is partially scrubbed to give you a before and after look.

Using a pot scrubbie, or a sanding sponge, scrape away the molds and dirt from the surface. Let dry.

Scrutinize the gourds for pits and marks or dark colorations. Although mottling is normal for gourds, a clear surface color is best if you want to put a face on the gourd.

Gourd Preparation

Although the gourds used in this book are ready to be used for our projects, let's review the path a gourd takes from the garden to the worktable. After a gourd has grown all summer, it will be ready to be harvested in the fall. The vine will die away and the fruit will be hanging, starting the next stage — dehydration. Dehydration is referred to by several names: drying-out, aging, curing, etc. No matter what term is applied, gourds are mostly moisture when the harvest begins and will lose about eighty-five percent of their body weight as they dehydrate before being used for gourd projects. Depending on the size of the gourd, that process can take two or more seasons. So, a gourd that has grown all summer, and was harvested after the vine had shown definite signs of dieback, will dehydrate until the next spring or summer...a year from seed to use.

Many people confuse the appearance of a de-hydrated gourd with rot because it will look dirty, molded, and frankly, pretty disgusting. Do not back down! As long as the gourd held its shape, is light for its size, and perhaps has the rattling sound of loose seeds when shaken, it is viable and ready to be cleaned up for art and craft purposes.

Let's quickly clean a gourd so you can see how to do it and can prepare your own stash for our projects.

Equipment

Here are two sets of 'equipment' used for the projects in this book: the "gourd-y" tools from the garage, and the supplies from the sewing room. These are the things from my house. Poke around your place and see what you have on hand before going out to buy new or expensive tools or supplies. My woodburners are purchased from the craft aisles of my local Wal-Mart and Miller Hardware stores. My fabrics are leftovers from quilting projects, and not originally purchased at full price (... gasp!). The weave is relatively tight so the stuffing material I use does not escape through the seams, or through the cloth weave. Large-weave cloth would not be suitable for stuffed dolls.

One thing I will caution you about is thread. Do not be cheap with thread. Get a good quality hand-quilting thread. It will make strong seams and not tangle too much as you sew, unlike a cheap five-for-a-dollar thread does. It is worth the investment.

Garage supplies: Sandblaster sandpaper, drill, cleaned miniature bottleneck gourds, gourd scraps, a coping saw blade clamped into the jaws of a locking wrench, woodburners equipped with a round and a chisel tip, a knife, branches, craft sticks, permanent markers, craft paints, toothpicks, spray lacquer, springs, a shop vac (not shown), latex gloves, wood glue, a bonding glue, hot glue gun, and glue stick.

Sewing rooms supplies: Cloth(s), sewing needles, hand-quilting threads, scissors, sewing machine, various kinds and colors of threads including a clear one that resembles fishing line, polyester fiber stuffing, notions for details like buttons, ribbon, do-dads, and a ruler.

Chapter Two:

Facial Features

It is normal to be all-thumbs when it comes to facial features, so leave behind any fears about artistry and talent. I am not a particularly good artist. Some of my dolls and puppets have no faces at all, just hairdos that have been made with a woodburner.

Here are the front of several dolls with no faces. I like the mystery facelessness offers.

The back view shows the variations of hairdos.

If you want a face, there are ways to get quick results by making simple shapes. You can practice these shapes and become quite proficient, perhaps even adding color or shading.

Let's try some facial features.

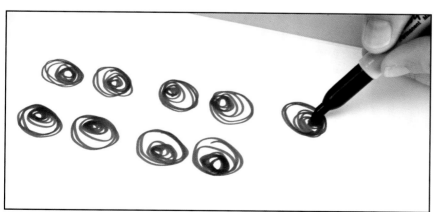

Eyes can be nothing more than a pair of spiraling circles. Using a permanent marker and a piece of scrap paper, practice making pairs of circles that start spiraling into themselves to make tight pupils.

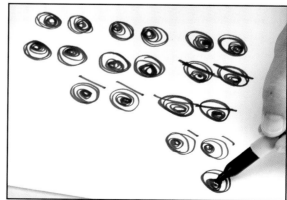

Depending on where you place the pupil inside the initial circle, the eyes can look into different directions. Simple lines serve as eyelids.

Another kind of a simple eye can be made with paint or markers. The same techniques apply either way although paint will have to dry between steps. Start with two sets of light blue circles for eyes, and then a darker blue circle on top of the first ones.

Make a dark half-moon line across the top of the circle so it extends beyond and down on both sides. I am using brown.

Add wispy lines for eyelashes at the bottom outside edges of the half-moon lines, and add brief arc lines over each eye for eyebrows.

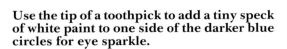

Use the tip of a toothpick to add a tiny speck of white paint to one side of the darker blue circles for eye sparkle.

For lips, make an elongated capital "M" so the tails splay in an outwardly direction.

Under and toward the center of the M, make a line in the shape of a half oval.

Color in the lips as you wish. Sometimes I leave them plain.

Chapter Three:

Hand Sewing

Because rag doll bodies involve sewing, many people will worry about seams and stitches and whether or not their sewing machine's tension is set correctly. Bottom line: As long as you can attach two pieces of cloth together in order to keep stuffing from escaping, you can make a doll body. Do not fret about specifics. A machine will certainly offer an element of speed if you want to make many dolls at once, but a sewing machine is not necessary to produce a doll body. You have a needle? You have thread? You can sew a durable doll body with the time-honored techniques of hand sewing.

Seamstresses have long used running stitches and backstitches to make seams — strong enough seams for men's pants and shirts! These stitches will be more than strong enough for our needs.

Definition of terms:

Running stitch — It's an up-and-down stitch making a line of thread connecting two pieces of cloth together.

Backstitches (also called locking stitches) — They're used to finish a line with a stitch that goes back over itself to resist unraveling.

Backstitching also produces a double line of stitches where extra strength might be necessary.

Hand sewing is meditative and worthwhile as a lap project while watching television or waiting for the kids at school.

Here is a quick lesson for hand sewing.

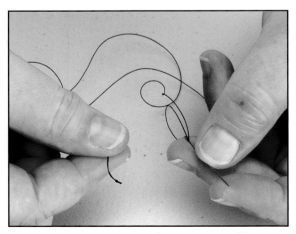
For a running stitch, thread a needle with about 24" of thread. Bring the ends together and knot.

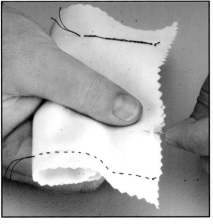
Starting near the end of the cloth, hold the cloth with one hand and push the point of the needle down into, and then up out of, the cloth.

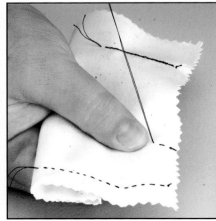
Repeat the down/up movements again, and pull thread all the way through the stitches.

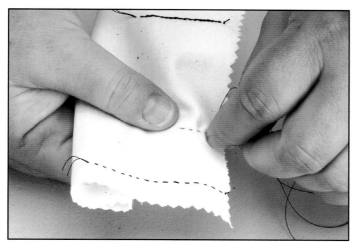

With small, close, up-and-down needle movements, make several stitches at once. Doing more than one stitch at a time will help you achieve a straighter line of sewing.

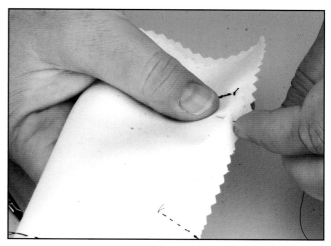

Backstitches are basically the same, except the needle backtracks over the previous stitch to make a double stitch. Make the first stitch as we did with the running stitch.

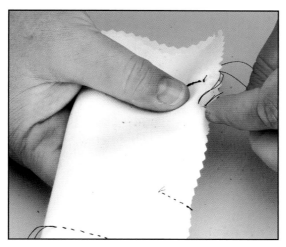

For the next stitch, place the point of the needle behind the spot where the thread is coming out of the cloth from the previous stitch.

Push the needle point into the cloth and then out of the cloth in front of the previous stitch.

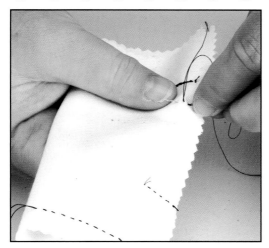

Pull thread through the cloth, and repeat the stitch by putting the point of the needle behind the spot where the thread is coming out of the cloth in the previous stitch.

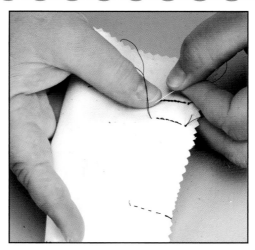

Backstitches are stronger than running stitches because they are double threaded, but they can only be made one at a time.

Chapter Four:

Rag Dolls

Floppy cloth dolls were probably called rag dolls because at one time the bodies were made from scraps of leftover cloth—rags—or perhaps the stuffing was old rags? I am not an historian, so I cannot offer details, but I remember rag dolls from my childhood, as do you I am sure.

Today, we are fortunate to have inexpensive cloth and assortments of plush fiber fillings available. Sometimes I use cottonballs for small dolls' arms and legs and I have been known to fill a gourd doll with rice or dried beans for a weightier and floppier doll body. However, some types of fill will work themselves through the weave of the cloth or seams, no matter how tightly woven the material or how tiny and perfect the seam stitches are, so think twice before you consider using sand, flour, or cornmeal. Natural products such as mints, roses, lavender, and cedar shavings make nice fill if you intend the doll to be a sachet and not handled a lot the way a play doll would be used from day to day.

The template produced for the rag doll in this book is based on the size of the gourds I have on hand that are, on average, 3" tall. The body is four times the size of the gourd, and the arm and leg widths are one and one-half (1 1/2) the size. This proportion seems to work for most gourds.

Let's make a gourd head and body.

To woodburn a faceless gourd head with a wavy hairdo, select a clear area where a face will not be distracted by a dark spot or wart mark. Make wavy lines along the sides of the face area. Stop the lines before reaching the curved area of the gourd.

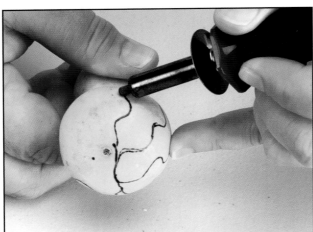

Turn the head around and make similar wavy lines in periodic places.

Keep turning the head and adding lines as the preliminary guidelines of the hairdo.

Back at the front, establish 'bangs' by burning curls at the hairline above the place where a face would be if you had one.

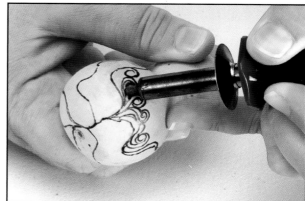

Fill in the spaces between the initial wavy lines to build hair all around. The lines will not be perfect reflections of each other, nor should you try to make them so. The variations will make the hair interesting.

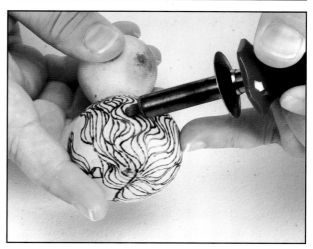

Sometimes you might get inspired to add a bow in an empty area, then burn the hair lines going toward the bow as if the hair has been bound together.

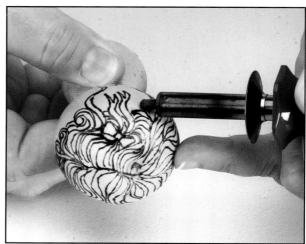

Once done with all the lines, you can leave the hair plain...

...or color the spaces with permanent markers to make a blonde, brunette, or redhead!

The beginning lines will determine the hairdo. Straight lines will give a bobcut style, and a part straight down the back will part the ways for ponytails.

After the head is done, spray it with lacquer lightly to seal it and give it some shine. If you want the original look of the raw gourd, but need protection, I encourage you to try one of the matte varnishes. MinWax makes a fast drying brush-on and spray-on polyurethane. Just remember, if you used color, apply any sealant with a light hand. Better to apply several thin coats, than one coat that makes the color bleed.

Usually, I make a whole bunch of heads at once. Then I can go from doll to doll with only minimal stops.

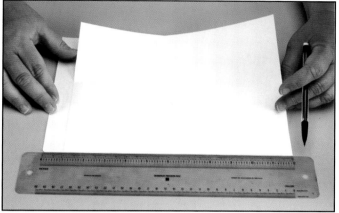

Now for the body: The gourds I have handy are about 3" tall. Our body template will be four times the gourd's size. I have two pieces of 8 ½" x 11" paper that have been placed and taped against each other to invent a 12" paper size.

With the papers sitting horizontal in front of you, mark two dots 1½" away from the bottom edge and use a pencil to draw a line connecting the dots, continuing to the ends of the paper on both sides. For convenience sake, we will call this the body line.

On the left side of the paper, mark two sets of dots: 1" and 2½" from the edge.

Still using a pencil, connect the dots with parallel lines that extend from the body line to the top edge of the paper. These lines will be the arms.

Measure three inches (gourd size) along the body line from the arm and make a dot. Label it "DB" (for Doll Body).

Move to the right side of the paper and mark two dots on the paper's edge: mark one dot ON the body line (labeled IDS for Inside Doll Leg), and mark the other dot 1 1/2" from the the body line (DL for Doll Leg).

Connect the "DB" line with the "DL" line.

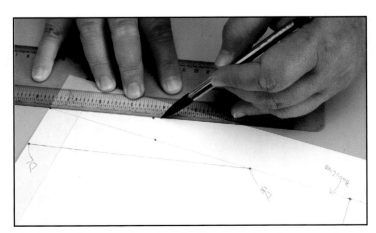

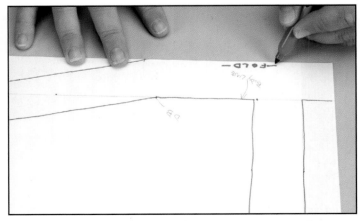

Halfway along, and under the line you just drew, mark a dot 1½" from the line. Draw a line from "IDL," through the dot you just marked, to the bottom edge of the paper. This is the second line of the leg.

Now, use a permanent marker or pen to trace the lines you will be cutting as shown. Mark the bottom edge of the paper with the word "Fold."

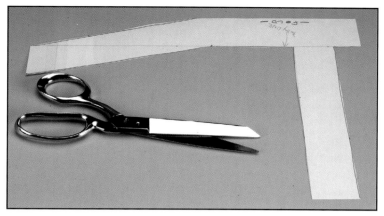

Tape the paper's edge that crosses the leg so it won't fall apart and cut out the template.

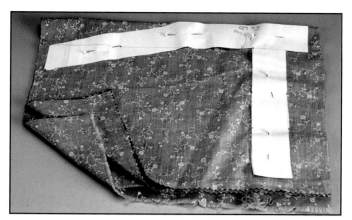

With the right sides (printed sides) together, fold two pieces of cloth and pin the template so the edge marked 'fold' aligns with the cloth fold.

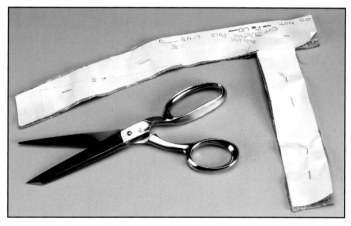

Cut on the lines, going through both pieces of cloth at once. Note: do not cut on the fold line.

Remove the pins and unfold the cloth to see the doll body. I like long arms and legs because I like to pose my dolls and put babies, buckets, and other props into their grasp. This is the time to trim them if you want them shorter.

Re-pin the body so you can sew it together. Make sure the cloth is arranged so the wrong side is out on both sides.

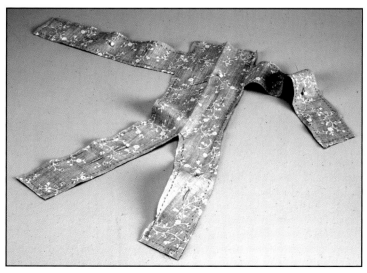

I made the sewing line obvious in this photo. It will be about a ¼" inside the cutting line.

Sew the body cloth together either with a machine...

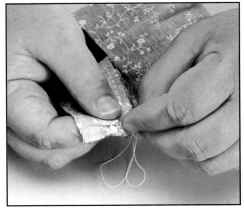

...or with hand sewing. Make back-stitches at the beginning, the corners, and at the end.

Make small snips at the right angles of the seam at the armpits and crotch to relieve tension. This will allow the cloth some 'give' when the body is turned inside out.

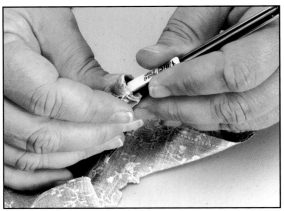

Turn the body inside out. I use a blunt-ended object like a capped pen or knitting needle and start at a foot, and push it into the body. Working the arms and legs in this fashion will eventually get the inside to the outside.

Since our doll is small, there is no real need to fill the legs and arms with filling. The bulk of the cloth will be adequate. Cut pieces of string and tie the ankle, knee, hip, wrist, elbow, and shoulder joints.

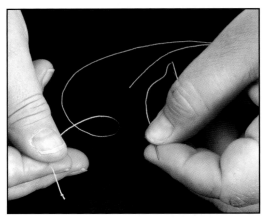

Thread a needle with about 24" of thread. Make a double-knot at one end.

Turn the neck edge over by ½" and finger-press the seam, so it tries to stay in place as you sew.

Beginning at the back of the neck, insert the needle into the cloth from the inside of the cloth so the knot is hidden.

Sew a running stitch around the neck a ¼" from the folded edge. Hand sewing at this time is best because you will eventually be pulling the thread and wrapping it around the neck, but you'll see that as we go along.

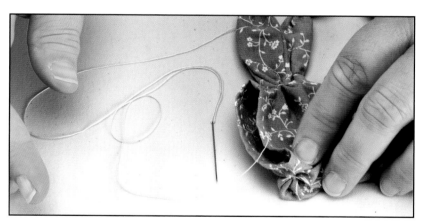

Leave the thread needle hanging when you return to the starting point.

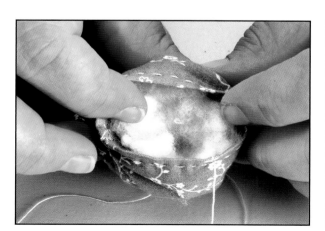

Stuff the body with polyester fill to the neck, leaving a hollow area in the fill for the bottom of the gourd.

Insert the bottom of a gourd head into the hollow area you left when filling the body. Make sure the fill surrounds the gourd bottom and is convincing as a body. The gourd should not be obvious from outside the body.

Cradling the doll body and gourd bottom, pull the threaded needle so the running stitch gathers the cloth at the neck.

Arrange the gathers in an evenly distributed fashion before pulling the thread tight.

Wrap the thread around the neck a couple times.

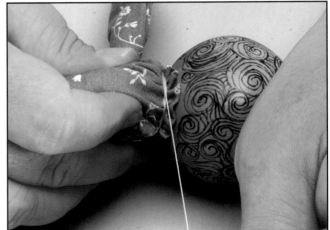

Sew a couple tiny stitches in one place and tie a knot. The repeated stitches bind the thread into a mass to resist unraveling should the knot come out.

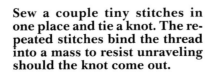

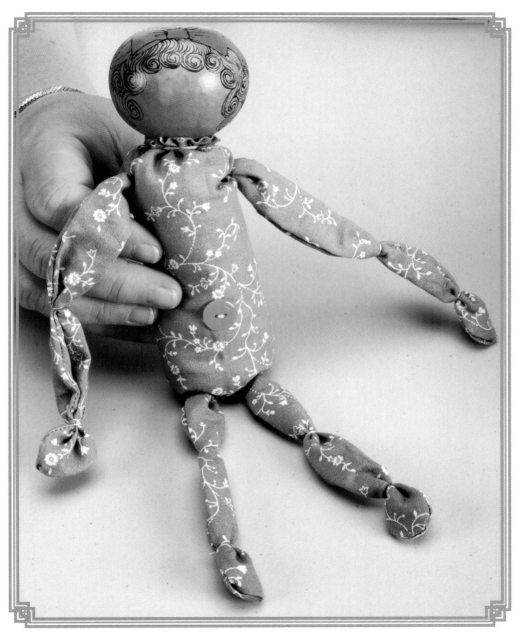

Decorate as you wish. I like belly buttons!

Marionette

A marionette is a rag doll with strings connected to key joints so movement is produced from afar to give the illusion the doll has a life of its own. I like to use clear thread or fishing line because the action seems more magical when the connections are not obvious. For teaching purposes, we will use string so you can see the lines and the connections. Marionettes can be very elaborate with a connector for every joint, but simple movement marionettes are with strings only to the hands, feet and head. Though we will make simple connections here, you will probably make spectacular examples of puppetry once you see how easy it can be. Just a little patience is all you need.

Let's make some simple connections!

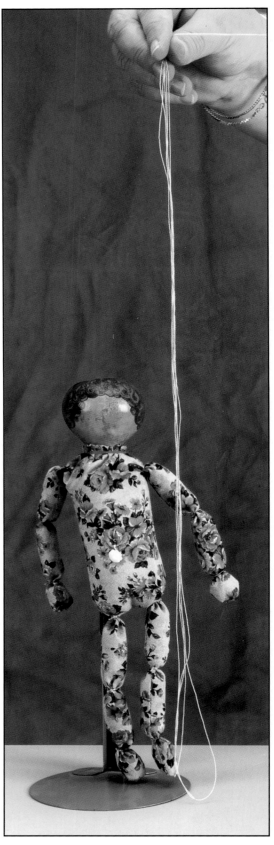

To begin, make a doll as we did earlier except use dried beans or lentils in the arms and legs for weight. Long arms and legs add additional space for movement.

Propping it up on a doll stand or some other innovation you may have, measure the approximate length of string you will need to reach from the feet to a comfortable grid height. This measurement is completely arbitrary according to personal taste. I am going with 2½ feet.

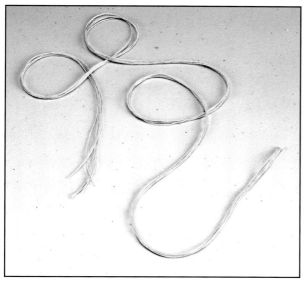

Cut five 5-feet lengths of thread. You will not need all of this for each appendage, but since it is easier to work with equally-sized pieces, a little waste is economical in the end.

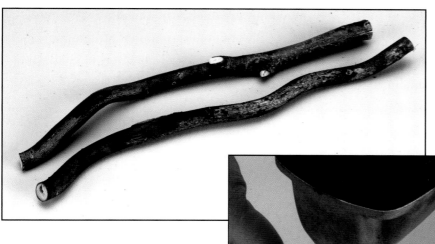

Cut two 8" branches to make the manipulation grid — I am using pieces of my curly willow tree. Dowels work, as do pieces of wood or plastic pipe.

About ½" from the ends of the branches, drill a hole big enough to pass a string through.

Cross the branches at mid-center and drill a hole.

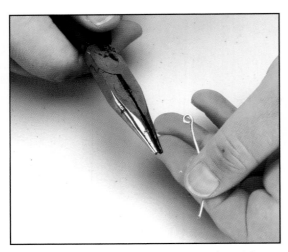

Cut a 2" piece of wire (I am using 16 gauge brass wire) and turn a small loop on one end with needle-nosed pliers.

Thread the wire through the center holes from the underside of the grid.

Turn another loop on top of the grid and settle it tightly against the branch by adjusting the loop's curve with the pliers.

Starting with the head, tie a piece of string to the grid's underside loop. Secure it with several tight knots.

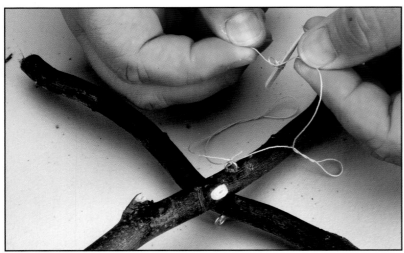

Measure about 18" along the line and tightly knot the string around a half piece of toothpick.

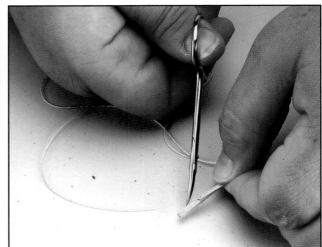

Trim the excess string.

Use a darning needle to pierce a hole in the top of the gourd head.

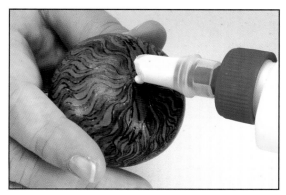

Squeeze wood glue into the hole...

...and insert the toothpick so it falls into the head. The glue will anchor it once it is inside and the glue dries.

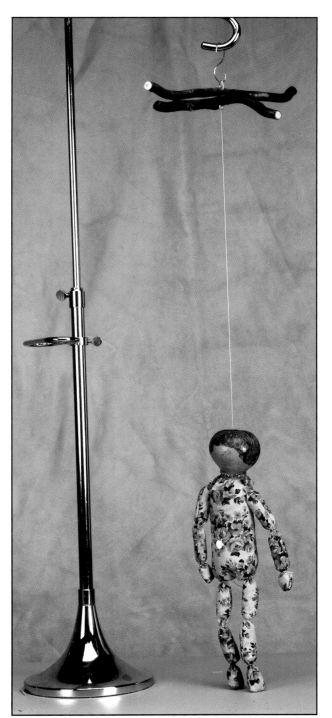

Hang the grid from something so the doll is suspended with its feet touching a surface.

Using a needle and thread, make several loops of thread in the same place to form a connector on the doll's backside.

Thread a length of string through the hole in the grid's branch behind the head. Tie several tight knots.

Thread the string through the connector loop at the doll's backside; pull the string taut until the doll spine is vertical.

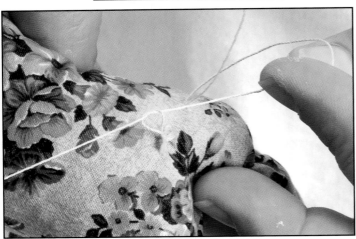

Knot the string tightly. Do not trim the ends until the very end in case adjustments are needed.

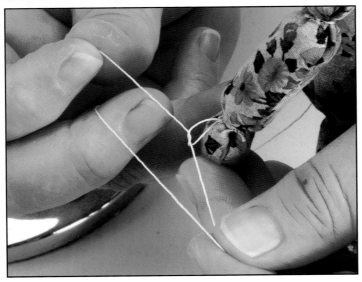

Tie the end of a length of string to one of the doll's wrists with several tight knots.

Thread the string through the hole in the branch on the same side of the grid.

Go through the head loop...

...and through the hole at the end of the branch that corresponds with the other arm.

Tie the string to the other wrist with several tight knots.

Check to see that the arms are just below the right angle of the body.

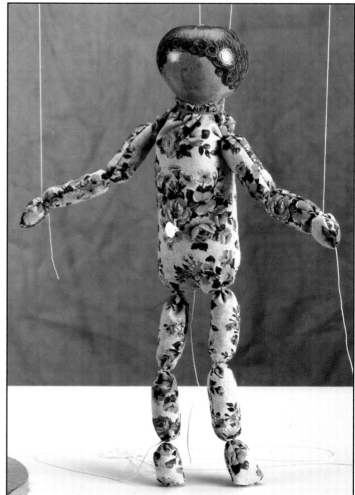

Thread the string through the hole on the front branch...

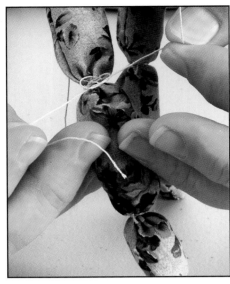

The knees are next. Attach a piece of string to the knee of one leg.

...and go through to the knee of the other leg.

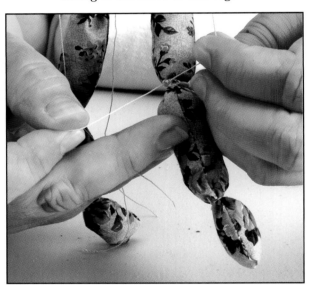

Tie tightly with several knots.

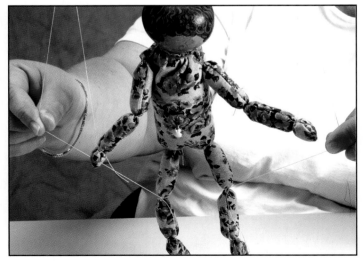

Bring the two leg strings out and around the arms and armstrings, to rest in position behind the elbows of the doll. Critique how everything hangs. You may need to adjust the lengths of the arms or legs. If so, cut the line and try again.

Trim all the string ends and dot the knots with glue.

Chapter Five

Flip-flop Dolls

Flip-flop gourd dolls have two heads so when the doll is turned upside-down there is a different doll face and therefore a different personality. Traditionally, dolls of this type had a ying/yang, opposite point of view from head to head: bride and groom, blonde and brunette, dog and cat, farmer and banker, etc. Give some pre-thought to the opposites you want to display for your two-head doll personalities because this may determine your choices of cloth and sewing notions (buttons, trim, etc.).

For a flip-flop doll, it will be important to choose a gourd with similar top and bottom belly sizes so the faces will only change design and colors, not size. Having said that, I have to admit I just thought about making a mother/child flip-flop where obviously the mother head would be bigger than the baby head — an example of the exception proving the rule of thumb!

Let's flip-flop!

For a flip-flop doll, choose a gourd with a similarly sized top and bottom bulge.

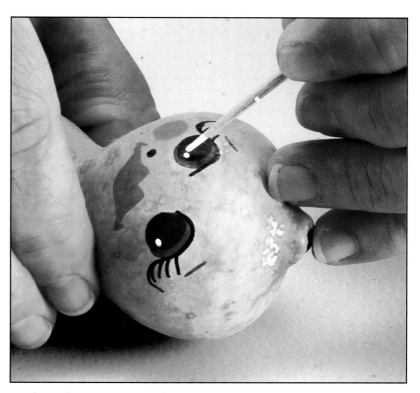

Make a face on one end. I'll make blue eyes and some lips as we made earlier in this book, with a mole over the lip and some blush

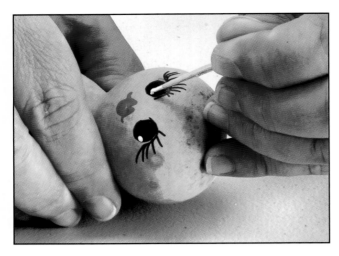

On the direct opposite end of the gourd, I'll do brown eyes with big eyelashes and a pouty mouth, which is the capital "M" and "U" technique we used earlier in the book, but fatter.

Spray lacquer or brush a thin coat of varnish by sitting the gourd in an egg carton and covering one side with a thin coat and let dry.

Turn the gourd over. Spray the other side with a thin coat of varnish and let dry. Repeat both sides again for added protection and shine.

Hair. Let's make one a blonde by cutting more than forty-eight pieces of yellow embroidery thread, each about 6" long.

Tie a 1/8" ribbon around one end to hold all the pieces together.

Use a piece of duct tape to secure the end to the table.

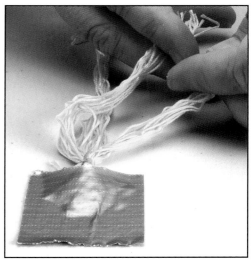

Divide the threads into three equal numbered sets.

Braid the sets by overlapping the left one over the middle one...

...and then the right one over the middle one ...

...and then back to the left one to start over again. Continue until the entire lengths have been braided.

Using another piece of ribbon, tie the ends together.

Run two 1" parallel lines of wood glue across the top of the gourd head that is no wider than the braid, and are running from 'ear to ear,' if there were ears.

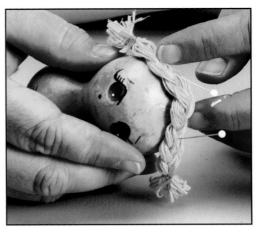

Center the braid over the head and glue and secure with a couple of straight pins so that it does not shift out of position until the glue dries.

The other end will be a brunette so, again, cut forty-eight or more strands of embroidery thread, but use dark colored thread.

To make a different hairstyle, use a piece of the same color embroidery thread and tie the middle of the threads together. Then spread the strings out in a circular fashion so all the threads radiate from the center.

Apply a dot of wood glue to the center of the opposite end of the gourd. About a ¼" from the dot, make a circle of wood glue.

Position the center of the circle of strings over the glue dot on the middle of the head, and radiate the threads evenly around the head over the circle of glue. Secure with straight pins so it will not shift out of position while it dries.

While the glue is drying, use scissors to clip the threads around the head into a straight bobcut. Start with the bangs...

...and continue trimming the threads around the head.

While everything dries thoroughly, select two different prints of cloth—one for each doll skirt—and cut two 5" x 8" pieces from each print.

Find some cloth for the arms and cut eight 1 ½" x 4" strips to make four sets of two.

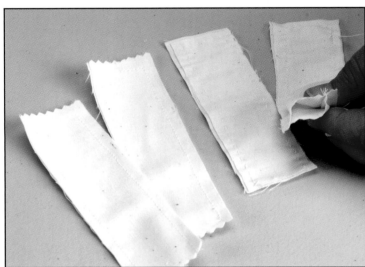

Sew each set together, leaving one of the short ends open. I have sown two sets with a machine and two sets by hand so you can see that both techniques work well.

Use an unsharpened pencil, or another blunt instrument, to turn the strips inside out by tucking the end inside itself and pushing the end inside until it emerges from the open end.

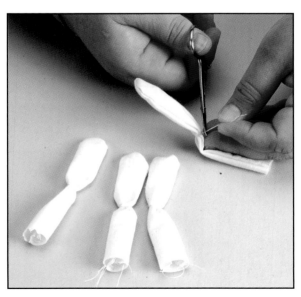

Tie thread around the elbow several times and knot. This gives the arm a natural bend. Trim the thread ends.

To make sleeves for one set of arms, cut two additional 2" x 3" pieces of the same skirt material used earlier; sew along the length, leaving both ends open and making a tube.

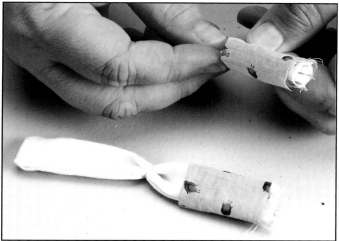

Fold half of the tube right side out and fit an arm into the tube so the open end of the arm aligns with the open end of the sleeve.

Make two sandwiches of the cloth you chose earlier: one 5" x 8" piece of cloth of each print. Put the right sides (the printed side) together.

Sew the pieces together along one of the long sides.

Open the cloth and iron flat. These are the skirt blocks.

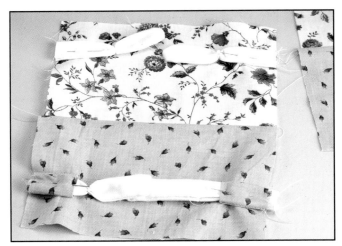
To give each doll arms, pin two arms to each cloth on one of the skirt blocks, about 1½" from the raw edge.

With the right sides and similar prints facing each other, put one cloth on top of the other so the arms are sandwiched inside.

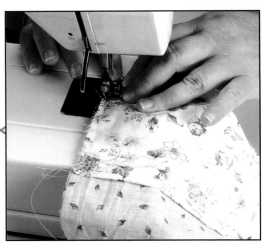
Sew the pieces together along the sides, catching the arms in the seam.

Turn one of the cloth prints to the outside to make a two-sided dress. The raw edges will align with each other with the wrong sides together.

Fold each raw edge ½" inward so the right sides are together. Pin in place.

As close to the edge as you can, sew the two-folded fabrics together. Make sure to backstitch when you return to the starting point to lock the stitches.

Move another ¼" from the first line and sew another line parallel to the first. Backstitch at the starting point.

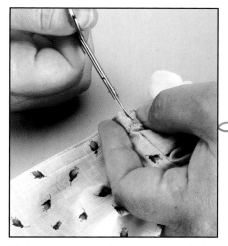

Using a seam ripper or cuticle scissors, carefully open a stitch or two at the side seam between the two lines to make a tiny entry hole.

Thread a blunt crewel needle with a 12" piece of 1/8" ribbon. Move the needle and ribbon through the parallel lines of sewing until you return to the opening from the other direction. The cloth will eventually be gathered with this ribbon.

Pull the needle through the hole and gather the cloth.

As the neck hole gets smaller, stop a moment to take the pins out of the now-dried hairdos and insert the gourd so the gathers are at the neck.

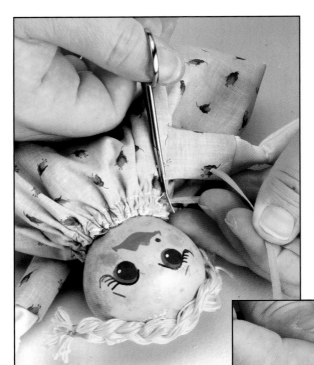

Pull the ribbon tightly and knot. Trim the ends.

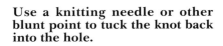

Use a knitting needle or other blunt point to tuck the knot back into the hole.

Flip the skirt dress over and add special decorative touches to the other side.

Add decorative touches to make this side of the doll unique.

Now, you have a gourd flip-flop doll. Here is one side...

...and here is the other side.

Chapter Six

Stick and Finger
Puppets

Once you have a gourd head made, it can be combined with arms and perhaps a costume to make a stick or finger puppet. Gather some head-sized gourds together and let's walk through several techniques for making stick and finger puppets.

Gather some small gourds together to make two kinds of gourd stick figures. Some of these gourds have been prepared as doll heads and some are plain.

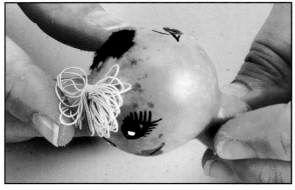

For the first stick puppet, choose a gourd with a face and hair on both the front and the back of the gourd.

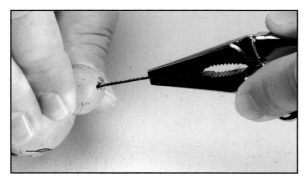

Cut a slit into the bottom of the gourd big enough to fit a craft stick for a handle.

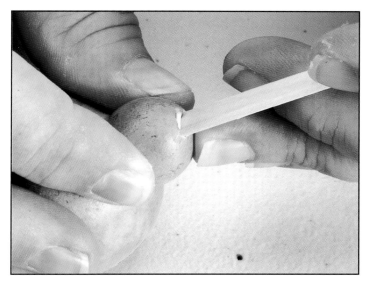

Squeeze wood glue into the stick and insert the stick handle. Let dry.

Using spray adhesive, attach images to neutral colored, stiff paper.

While the gourd and stick are drying, get a department store catalog and tear out some pages that show clothes models that are about the same size, possibly with similar poses.

Cut out the images, removing the heads.

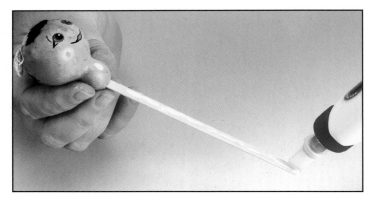

Run a thin line of glue along the craft stick, and one dot of glue under the "throat" of the gourd head.

Put the paper body in place. Pin the 'throat' to the glue dot. Hold the stick and paper body until the glue sets.

Turn the stick over, and repeat the procedure with the second paper body.

Now you have a person.

Turn the stick, and there is another person. A puppet show in the making!

Another puppet—or maybe it's a doll—is a stick figure using wire. Choose a gourd. I am using mini-kettle gourd here, turned sideways so the top is the nose.

Unwind about 6" of wire. I am using 16 gauge brass wire.

Twist the end into the top of the gourd head. Push and twist it through and out the bottom. Leave about 7" extending from the top of the head.

Bend the top piece of the wire behind and down the backside of the head to the neck area where the other end of wire comes through the gourd.

Twist the two ends a couple times to make a neck. You may need to tweak the wire at the back of the head to tighten it against the gourd.

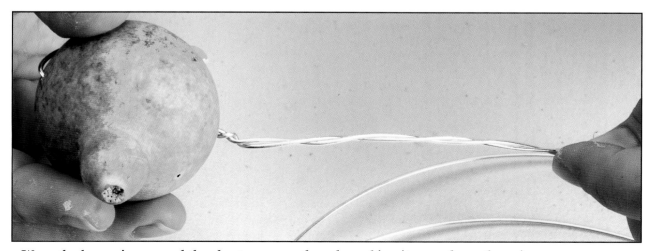

Wrap the long wire around the shorter one as though working its way down the spine.

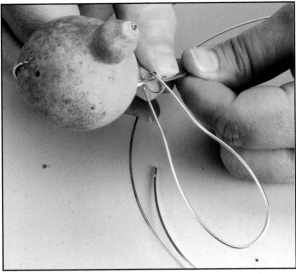 

Move back up the spine to the shoulders and wrap the wire around the shoulder area twice, making a 3" arm loop on one side of the shoulders.

Wrap the wire around the shoulders again, and extend it to the other side to make another arm loop.

Wrap once more around the shoulders before heading down the spine to wrap the hips a couple of times.

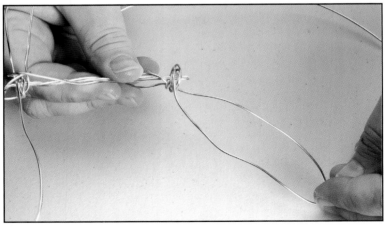

Extend down one hip to make a leg loop.

Wrap the hips again before extending down the opposite side to make another leg loop.

After getting back to the hips, wrap two or three times, and cut wire. Bend the end into the tangle of wire at the hips.

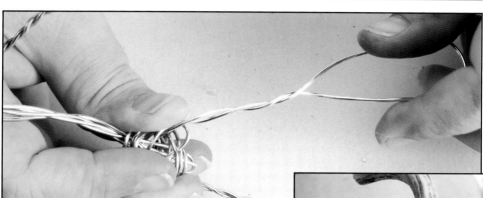

The arm and leg loops are twisted, leaving ovals at the ends for hands and feet.

These stick figures can be shaped into all sorts of whimsical poses. I used them for inexpensive art models when I was in school. Of course, that might be why I am not a particularly good artist!

Finger puppets are a little different. They are gourd heads with either a hole in the bottom so they can be placed on a finger; or, a gourd scrap with a hollow-space big enough for a finger.

Choose a head and drill a hole in the bottom.

Empty the debris by shaking it out, or using tweezers to pull out larger pieces.

Finger holes will be various sizes, depending on drill bit or scrap. To enlarge a hole, roll sandpaper around a pen or pencil and abrade the inside diameter.

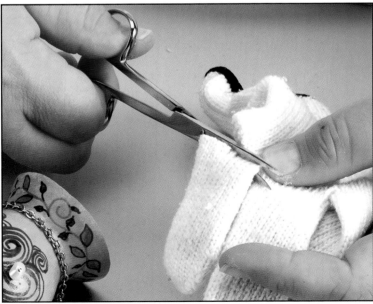

If the hole is larger than your finger, cut off the finger of an old glove, and insert it into the gourd.

Glue the edges of the glove finger to the inside of the gourd.

48

Sock Puppets

Sock puppets are the common hand puppets most people remember from their childhoods. Using an old sock, added pieces of gourd not only gives the sock some fun personality, but uses up gourd scraps. This is a particularly good project for children since gourd scraps and permanent markers are the basis for the adornments. Simplicity at its best!

Grab a sock and some gourd scraps!

Our gourd sock puppet is going to have eyes and big goofy teeth that are made from the circle scraps that result when opening birdhouse gourds. These are 7/8" disks with a 3/16" center hole.

Scrape and sand the backs of the scraps to remove the left-over debris and pith from the inside of its original gourd.

Sand the rough edges of the scrap. Two circles will become the goofy front teeth, so sand a little more off three sides of those circles so the teeth have a rounded bottom, but flatter sides and top.

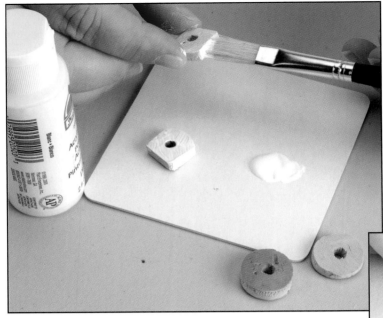

Paint the two tooth circles white. I am using craft paint.

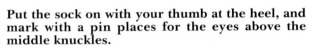

Because the disk has a center hole, use hot glue to cover the hole with a button. I have selected two buttons that are bigger than the hole in the disk.

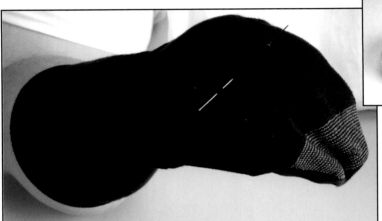

Put the sock on with your thumb at the heel, and mark with a pin places for the eyes above the middle knuckles.

Remove the sock from your hand, and hot glue the scraps to the sock.

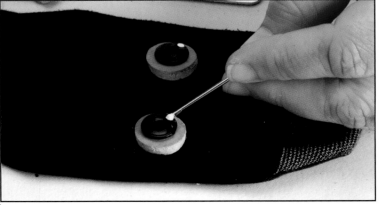

Place a small dot of white paint on each button 'pupil' to give that extra sparkle.

By now the teeth are dry. Put on the sock and mark with a pin the place you want the teeth, usually behind the place where the middle finger pushes at the toe of the sock.

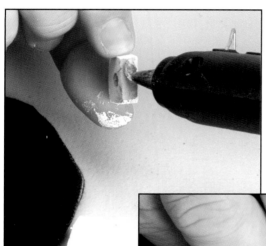

Using a hot glue gun, run a line of glue across the flat top part of a tooth...

...and without hesitation, press the tooth into place. Hold it until the glue has soaked into the threads of the sock and cools.

Do the same with the other tooth.

We'll make a hat for our sock puppet. Use something to trace a 3-1/2" circle onto some stiff paper. I am using two-sided scrapbook paper.

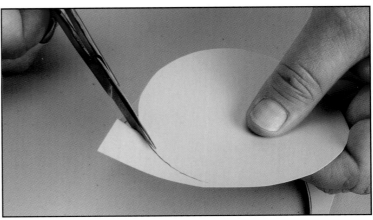

Cut out the circle.

On the back side of the paper, divide the circle into thirds with light pencil lines and make a 1" slit in the center of the lines.

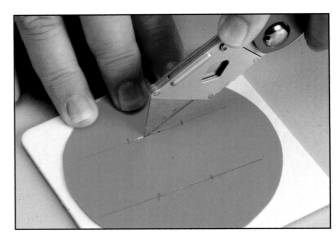

Using a ribbon that is about 1" wide and perhaps 18" long, go from the back side through one slit, over the top and down through the other slit. Pull the ribbon ends so they are equal in length.

On the back side, run a line of hot glue along the slit to anchor the ribbon and reinforce the paper.

Tie the ribbon ends together into a bow that will flop around when the sock is on a hand.

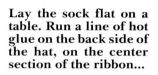

Lay the sock flat on a table. Run a line of hot glue on the back side of the hat, on the center section of the ribbon...

...and quickly press behind the eyes and over the wrist. Let the glue cool for couple moments.

Add some decoration to the hat, and — Voilá!

Bobble Heads

Bobble heads are fun, and will one day be a book all by themselves! Here is a beginning gourd bobble head to wet your whistle. Note: Springs can be bought in many, many sizes and states of limberness at a good hardware store. My local Ace Hardware has drawers of springs of various sizes and tensions. Larger gourds will require a hardier spring than a mini-bottleneck gourd, and it is nice to have the choices a well-stocked shop can offer.

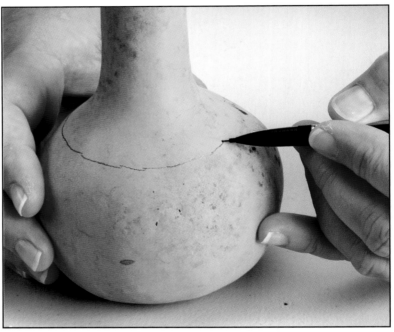

Select a gourd with a bulbous bottom. It doesn't matter what kind of gourd because you only want the rounded belly part before the wall curves for the stem or handle.

Just before the curve at the neck, hold a pencil point against the gourd and turn the gourd around to draw a line around the gourd.

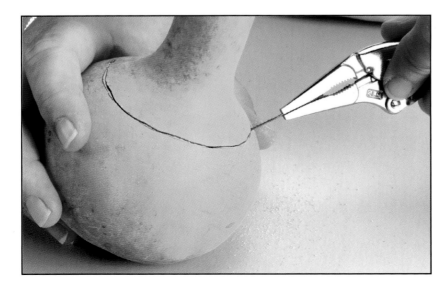

Cut the gourd open along the line. I'm making an entry hole with a darning needle and am using a coping saw blade in the jaws of a locking wrench... one of my favorite homemade tools.

Once open, empty the debris and use a grapefruit spoon, or any scraping tool, to encourage get the interior pith and seeds to release.

Vaccum any loose dust and particles from the gourd interior.

Sand the edge smooth. I sand near the vacuum nozzle.

Decorate the head as you see fit. I am using lamb's wool for the hair...

...and Sharpies for the face.

Spray the head with a thin coat of lacquer. Let dry and spray again.

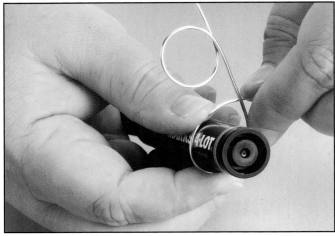

To make eyeglasses, wrap wire around a marker pen, in two loops, and bend the ends backwards.

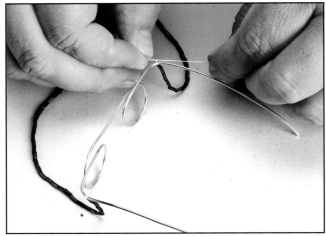

Tie a thread of bugle beads onto the sides of the eyeglasses for a movable decoration.

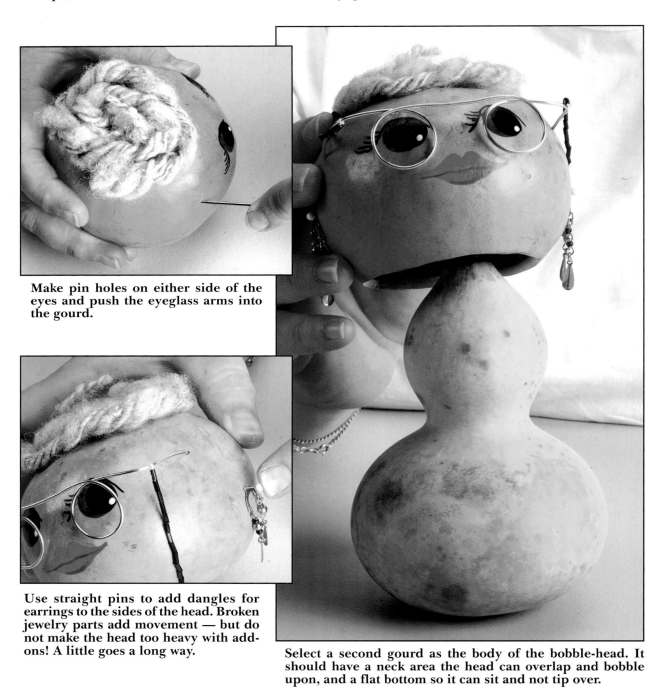

Make pin holes on either side of the eyes and push the eyeglass arms into the gourd.

Use straight pins to add dangles for earrings to the sides of the head. Broken jewelry parts add movement — but do not make the head too heavy with add-ons! A little goes a long way.

Select a second gourd as the body of the bobble-head. It should have a neck area the head can overlap and bobble upon, and a flat bottom so it can sit and not tip over.

Select a spring with some limberness. For a small gourd head, a ¼" x 1 1/16" spring usually works fine. Larger gourds will need more strength. The spring should be a little shorter than the gourd head interior.

Turn the head over and prop it up so the bottom is level.

Squeeze a little hill of hot glue in the center of the gourd bottom.

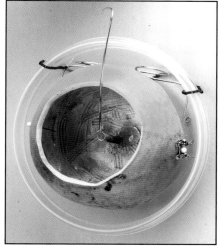

Situate the spring into the glue, and hold it in position for several minutes, until the glue cools and hardens.

On the second gourd, draw some clothes to match the gourd head's personality. I will start with a neckline collar.

On one side, draw an arm that goes towards the center front.

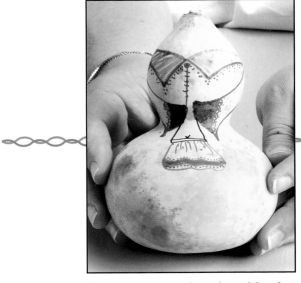

Draw an arm on the other side, that goes towards the center front where the rounded hands are holding a purse.

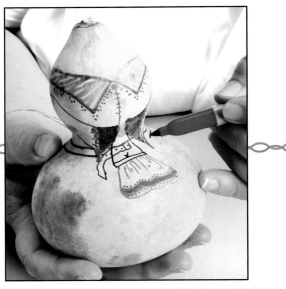

After the arms are in place, a horizontal line goes around the belly for a belt.

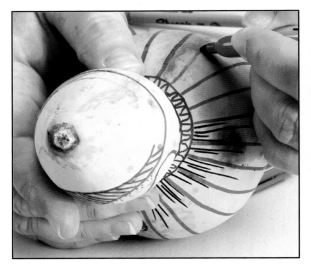

Lines are drawn on the skirt for pleats.

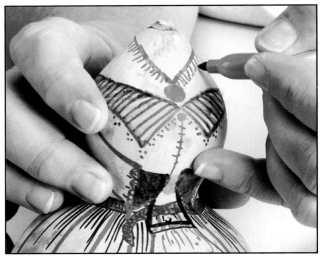

Some little frilly details are added.

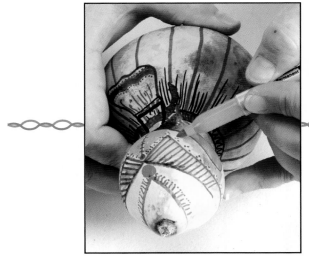

Color.

A couple thin coats of spray lacquer or polyurethane are applied

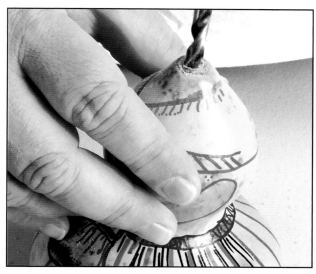

Once dry, the stem is broken off if it is not already gone, and a shallow hole is drilled at the stem base where the gourd wall will be thickest. The hole should be a tight fit for the end of the spring.

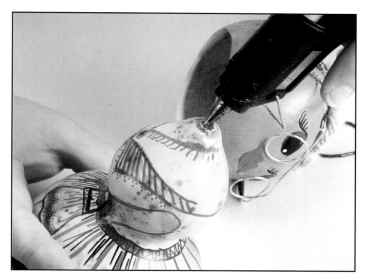

Hot glue is put into the hole.

Quickly place the head, with spring, onto the body. Hold in position several minutes, until the glue hardens and cools. Let it dry for several hours, or overnight for complete strength.

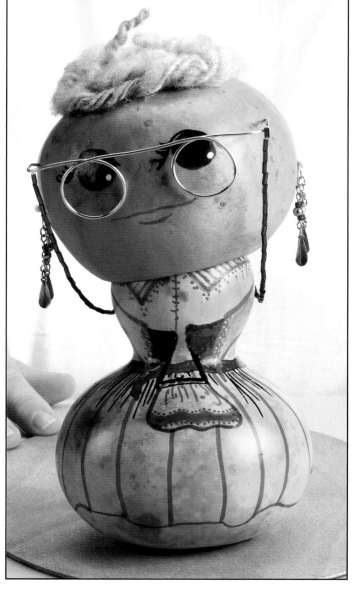

Once dry, we're bobbling! Note: some constructions are top-heavy, and may require a base.

Concluding Words

By now you have a nice overall view of gourd dolls and puppets...a terrific basis from which to build your own ideas. Believe me, as you work on one project, ideas for others will come to mind. Keep a notebook handy to jot down project thoughts as they come to you, either in total, or even as pieces of ideas. Sometimes the better projects come together only after small pieces are jotted down and the pattern emerges!

Join your state chapter of the American Gourd Society. There is nothing like meeting with other like-minded folks to indulge in the wealth and sheer joy of making something from nature. Start your own local 'gourdpatch' with friends or neighbors! When ideas get bounced around, they grow and just keep getting better and better.

Have fun, have joy, and keep gourding!

Angela

Gallery

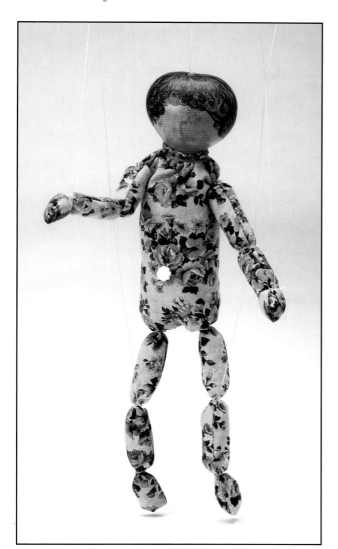

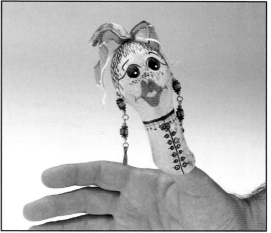

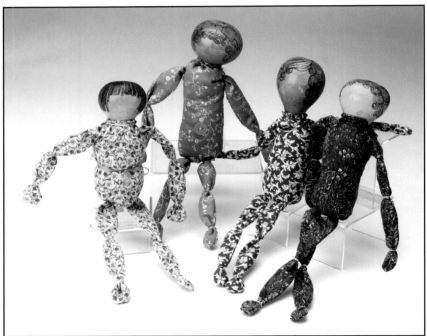

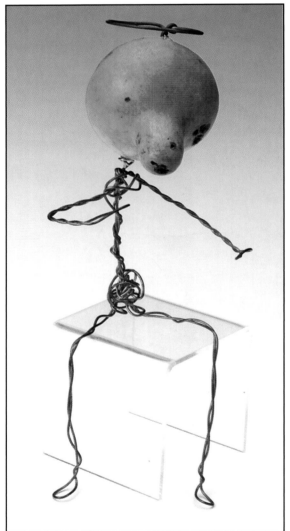

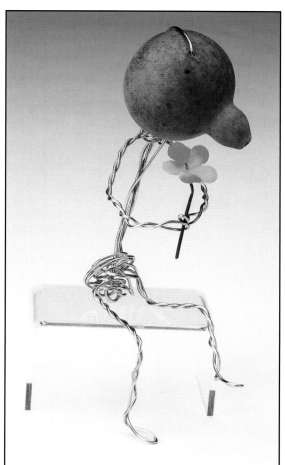